Unsolved Mysteries

Where Was Atlantis?

Brian Innes

RSVP
RAINTREE
STECK-VAUGHN
P U B L I S H E R S
A Steck-Vaughn Company

Austin, Texas

Developed by Brown Partworks
Editor: Lindsey Lowe
Designer: Joan Curtis

Raintree Steck-Vaughn Publishers Staff
Project Manager: Joyce Spicer
Editor: Pam Wells

Library of Congress Cataloging-in-Publication Data
Innes, Brian.
    Where was Atlantis?/by Brian Innes.
        p.   cm.—(Unsolved mysteries)
    Includes bibliographical references and index.
    Summary: Discusses the legend of the lost civilization of Atlantis and
whether it may have been based on a real place.
    ISBN 0-8172-5476-5 (Hardcover)
    ISBN 0-8172-4273-2 (Softcover)
    1. Atlantis—Juvenile literature. [1. Atlantis.] I. Title. II. Series: Innes,
Brian. Unsolved mysteries.
    GN751.I55   1999
    001.94—dc21   98-3389
                                                              CIP
                                                               AC

Printed and bound in the United States
1 2 3 4 5 6 7 8 9 0 WZ 02 01 00 99 98

Acknowledgments

Cover Jeremy Walker/Tony Stone Images;
Page 5: Tony Arruza/Corbis; **Pages 6 and 7:**
William M. Donato/Fortean Picture Library;
Page 9: NASA/Science Photo Library; **Page 10:**
Mary Evans Picture Library; **Page 11:** Fate
Magazine/Mary Evans Picture Library; **Page 13:**
Dave Houser/Corbis; **Page 15:** Mary Evans Picture
Library; **Page 16:** Gianni Dagli Orti/Corbis;
Page 17: Francesco Venturi/Kea Publishing
Services/Corbis; **Page 19:** Sergio Dorantes/Corbis;
Page 20: Mireille Vautier; **Page 21:** Hulton-Getty;
Page 23: Wolfgang Kaehler/Corbis; **Page 24:**
NRSC Ltd./Science Photo Library; **Page 25:** Mary
Evans Picture Library; **Page 26:** Fortean Picture
Library; **Page 27:** AKG, London; **Page 28:** Fortean
Picture Library; **Page 31:** John Beatty/Tony Stone
Images; **Page 32:** Erich Lessing/AKG, London;
Page 33: Collection Antochiw/Mireille Vautier;
Page 34: Corbis-Bettmann; **Page 36:** Adam
Woolfitt/Corbis; **Page 37:** Michael Diggin;
Page 38: Adam Woolfitt/Corbis; **Page 41:** Kevin
Schafer/Corbis; **Page 43:** Gary Braasch/Corbis;
Page 44: Gail Mooney/Corbis; **Page 46:** Wolfgang
Kaehler/Corbis.

Contents

City Under the Sea

Nearly 30 years ago something amazing was found under the sea. Was it the lost city of Atlantis?

In September of 1968, an archaeologist named Dr. J. Manson Valentine visited the Bahamas, which is a chain of small islands that lies off the coast of Florida. One day, a local guide called Bonefish Sam took Dr. Valentine to an area that was known to be good for fishing. This was just off the northwest coast of a small island known as North Bimini. What Dr. Valentine saw that day amazed him. Below, in about 25 feet (7.5 m) of water, was a line of huge stones. It was like a highway under the sea.

AN IMPORTANT DISCOVERY

Dr. Valentine was a professor at the Museum of Science in Miami, Florida. He had been on archaeological expeditions to the South Pacific and to the Yucatán Peninsula in Mexico. He was interested in lost civilizations and had spent 15 years in the Bahamas searching for traces of people who had lived there long ago. Now he was sure he had made an important discovery.

In a report, Dr. Valentine said that the line of stones under the sea near North Bimini was nearly 700 yards (640 m) long. He described them as "an extensive pavement of regular . . .

The calm, emerald green waters off the island of North Bimini (opposite) revealed an amazing secret in September 1968.

4

"A portion of the temples
may yet be discovered
under the slime of ages of
seawater near Bimini."

EDGAR CAYCE

The Bimini Road. Some stones were rounded off (top), while others looked as if they had been cut into squares (above).

flat stones, obviously shaped and accurately aligned [lined up]." Dr. Valentine went on to report that the stones must have been under the water for a long time. "The edges of the biggest ones had become rounded off, giving the appearance of . . . loaves of bread, or pillows of stone."

Many people were excited by the news of the "Bimini Road." However, a year later John Hall, a professor of archaeology at the University of Miami, took a team of divers on a trip to look at it. He reported back that, "we found no evidence whatsoever of any work of human hand . . . ." Other archaeologists, however, were not so sure.

THE SEARCH CONTINUES

In 1975, a team of experts set out to make a full survey of the Bimini Road. They found that the stones ran in a straight line for about 1 mile (1.6 km). Then they curved around and ran for at least another 800 yards (730 m). Most of the Bimini Road was made from huge stone blocks, each one about 17 x 17 feet (5 x 5 m), and more than 3 feet (1 m) thick. Strangest of all was the discovery of a piece of stone with a tongue-and-groove joint—one piece slotting tightly into another. The team could tell that it had been worked by human hands.

Could these strange stone remains be those of a city under the sea? John Steele, a member of the 1975 expedition, has explained that the sea around the Bahamas rose steadily from the end of the last ice age—around 10,000 B.C. This suggested that the stones of the "road" would have been more than 30 feet (9 m) above sea level in 6000 B.C., but nearly 10 feet (3 m) below the water by 2000 B.C.

It was not surprising that people imagined the Bimini Road to be part of the lost city of Atlantis. And then someone remembered what the American psychic Edgar Cayce had said about Atlantis in 1933: "A portion of the temples may yet be discovered under the slime of ages of seawater near Bimini. Expect it in '68 or '69—not so far away."

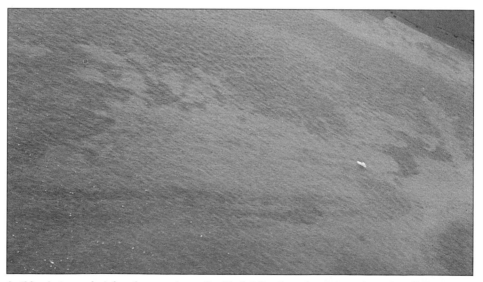

In this photograph, taken from a plane, the Bimini Road can be seen underwater off the Bahamas. The small white speck (center right) is a boat anchored over one end of the "road."

7

The Story of Atlantis

According to legend, Atlantis was an island that vanished beneath the waves many thousands of years ago.

An aerial picture, taken from space (opposite), of the Strait of Gibraltar. This is the narrow passage of water that lies between the Mediterranean Sea (top) and the Atlantic Ocean (bottom).

The Greek philosopher Plato, who lived about 2,350 years ago, gave the first written account of Atlantis. He said this story originally came from an elderly priest from Egypt. Plato wrote that Atlantis had existed nearly 10,000 years before his own time. It was a huge land, "bigger than North Africa and Asia put together."

The ancient Greeks were sailors, but they sailed only in the Mediterranean Sea. At the western end of the Mediterranean, between Spain to the north and Morocco to the south, is a narrow passage of water. This is called the Strait of Gibraltar. The ancient Greeks called it the Pillars of Hercules. Beyond lay a vast, unexplored ocean. Plato wrote that, "Once upon a time, the land of Atlantis lay somewhere in this ocean." He said that is why it was named the Atlantic Ocean.

LAND OF PLENTY

We can imagine that Atlantis was an island continent like Australia. It could have been about the same size. Plato wrote that every type of plant grew there, providing food, and lumber for building. There were herds of all kinds of

8

"Once upon a time,
the land of Atlantis lay
somewhere in this ocean."

PLATO

animals, and the earth was full of metals that could be mined. One of these was called "oreichalk." It was nearly as precious as gold.

Atlantis was the richest land ever known. The capital city was built on a mountain. It was surrounded by three moats, large ditches of water dug by hand, one inside the other. To protect the city, huge stone walls were built on the land between each moat. The outermost wall was covered with bronze, the middle wall with tin, and the inner wall with oreichalk. Plato said the last wall "sparkled like fire."

THE GOLDEN YEARS

A great temple stood in the center of the city. It was surrounded by a wall of gold. The outside of the temple was covered with silver, and the roof was made from solid ivory. Inside the temple were golden statues of the kings and queens of Atlantis. There was also a huge statue of Poseidon, god of the sea. It was nearly 300 feet (91 m) high and was made from solid gold. The royal palace was near the temple. This was surrounded by beautiful gardens.

On the islands between the moats were other temples. The king who ruled this wonderful royal city was the most important man in the land, but there were nine other cities

Poseidon (left) was the Greek god of the sea. Statues of him would have been worshiped by the people of Atlantis.

This Fate *magazine cover from July 1953 shows what everyday life may have been like on Atlantis.*

on Atlantis. Each was ruled by its own king. All 10 kings met every few years to agree on the island's laws. At these meetings they sacrificed a bull to Poseidon.

A vast plain lay beyond the royal city. It was crossed by a number of rivers that flowed to the sea. In the nearby mountains the country folk lived in many wealthy villages.

In the beginning, according to Plato, the Atlanteans—the people of Atlantis—had everything they could possibly need. But as time went on they became greedy for more power. The fighting force of Atlantis was one of the biggest the world has ever known. In the royal city alone there were 60,000 "captains" who were each able to raise a huge army from the people of the surrounding countryside. There was an enormous force of 10,000 chariots, and the royal navy had over 1,000 galleys, a type of wooden ship powered by oars. With their army, the kings of Atlantis captured lands as far east as Egypt and as far north as Tuscany in Italy.

SUDDEN DISASTER

Plato wrote that Zeus, king of all the gods, decided to punish the people of Atlantis for their greed—and there Plato's story breaks off. However, we do know a little more from a short account that he had written earlier: "There came violent earthquakes and floods. In a single dreadful day and a single dreadful night, the island of Atlantis was swallowed up by the sea."

Before the Flood

In the late 19th century, the story of the lost world of Atlantis became a popular legend.

For several centuries, scholars thought Plato's account of Atlantis was pure fiction. But some people wondered if it had any connection with the story of the Great Flood, as described in ancient legends throughout the world.

When sailing ships could be built large and strong enough, sailors began to explore the Atlantic Ocean. They found islands—Madeira, the Azores, the Canaries—and thought these might be the mountain peaks of the lost land of Atlantis. Some explorers went farther west, and discovered that there was a vast continent on the far side of the ocean.

A NEW CONTINENT

Perhaps this continent was what remained of Atlantis? Certainly some mapmakers thought so. They named the new land "Atlantis," even though the Italian sailor Amerigo Vespucci had already given it his own name, "America."

When Spanish explorers met the Aztecs, who were the native people of Mexico, the theory that Atlantis had been destroyed by the Great Flood seemed to be proven. These peoples had a legend that they originally came from a place

The Aztec people built pyramids that were similar to those found in Egypt (opposite).

"They built pyramids that were similar to those found in Egypt."

called Aztlan. They built pyramids that were similar to those found in Egypt. Following the discovery of America, many Europeans decided that Plato's story of Atlantis might be true after all. For several centuries afterward, even many respected scientists thought so, too. Then, in 1882, Ignatius Donnelly published his book *Atlantis*. He wrote about the time before the legendary Flood.

A MAN OF IDEAS

Ignatius Donnelly was born in Philadelphia in 1831. He studied law. In 1856, he relocated to Minnesota. In 1859, at the age of 28, he was elected lieutenant governor of Minnesota. Donnelly ran twice for vice president of the United States. When he lost for the second time, in 1870, he retired from politics and became an author.

" . . . many Europeans decided that Plato's story of Atlantis might be true."

Atlantis was Donnelly's first book, and it was a great success. It has since been printed more than 50 times. He followed it with *Ragnarok: the Age of Fire and Ice*. In this second book, Donnelly argued that the ice age had been caused by the collision of Earth with a huge comet.

Donnelly's description of Atlantis steadily grew in popularity. In his book *Atlantis*, he began by stating 13 propositions, or statements of opinion. The first four claimed that what Plato had described was true.

This map shows the possible position of the continent of Atlantis during the ice age. One theory is that when the ice finally melted, its waters flooded Atlantis.

Atlantis had been a huge landmass. It occupied much of the space between Europe and the Americas. The fifth statement claimed that Atlantis was "antediluvian," a term that is used to describe the period of history before the Flood. It was the real Garden of Eden, as well as all the other Paradises described in the religious traditions of nations all over the world.

A FORGOTTEN CIVILIZATION

Donnelly's sixth and seventh statements claimed that the gods of ancient Egypt, Greece, Phoenicia, India, Scandinavia, and Peru were really the remembered kings and queens of Atlantis. The stories told about them were variations of true events.

Donnelly's next four statements suggested that Atlantis was the real root of modern civilization. He claimed that the people of Atlantis had taken bronze to Europe and were the first workers in iron. The Phoenician alphabet, which was the basis of the Greek alphabet, had come from Atlantis. This alphabet was also taught to the Mayan peoples of Central America. Many of the different races of the world were also said, by Donnelly, to be descended from Atlanteans.

In his final statements, Donnelly repeated Plato's description of the end of Atlantis. Then, he wrote, "A few persons escaped in ships and on rafts, and carried, to the nations east and west, tidings of the appalling catastrophe [stories of the terrible disaster], which have survived to our own time in the Flood and Deluge legends of the different nations of the old and new worlds."

FINDING THE PROOF

This was, certainly, an interesting theory. Donnelly then set out to "prove" it. He pointed out that there was nothing impossible in Plato's story. There was no "science fiction." Continents have risen and sunk in the course of Earth's history. Everyone knows that islands have been formed and others destroyed during volcanic eruptions. And around the Azores, exactly in the spot where Plato had placed the island of Atlantis, the ocean is not very deep. This area is called the Atlantic Ridge.

So far, Donnelly's argument was sound. But then there were the mummies of Egypt and Peru. Donnelly thought that they were similar. In both

This is a Peruvian mummy from about 700 B.C. It is wrapped in an embroidered cloth.

Ceremonies were held in the temple at the top of the Mayan pyramids. This one is at Chichén Itzá, Mexico.

countries the air is very dry, and dead bodies can be kept from decaying. However, the Egyptians removed all the internal organs, and the bodies were laid out flat before they were wrapped up. The Peruvians wrapped the whole of the body in a crouching position.

And as for the ancient pyramids of Egypt and Central America, they are only roughly similar in shape. All the sides of the Egyptian pyramids are sloped. They were built as burial places. The Mayan pyramids have steps that lead up to a temple. There, sacrifices and other religious ceremonies were performed.

A COMMON LANGUAGE

The final proof, Donnelly wrote, could be found in language. He claimed that much of the Mayan language was pure Greek. He said another language of Central America was like Hebrew, and a third was similar to Chinese. Experts who study the history of languages say these claims are quite untrue.

Donnelly's book was all theory. He was trying to explain why he thought Plato's story of Atlantis and its destruction could be true. Unfortunately, most of the statements of "fact" that Donnelly used in his argument were wrong. But this did not stop other writers from telling even more fantastic stories.

The Legend Grows

Tales of volcanic eruptions and floods fueled interest in the great legend of Atlantis.

A few years before Ignatius Donnelly published his book on Atlantis in 1882, a Frenchman named Charles-Etienne Brasseur became interested in the peoples of South America and the Mayan alphabet. Only three Mayan books exist, although there are also inscriptions, or writings, on various monuments. However, at that time nobody understood the inscriptions.

Brasseur decided that the books were about a huge volcanic eruption in an unknown land. This was followed by a great flood. He came to the conclusion that the name of the land was Mu. However, it is now known that Brasseur's understanding of the Mayan alphabet was wrong. Experts have since translated large portions of the books, and they seem to be mostly about astronomy, the study of the stars and planets.

As interest in the island of Atlantis grew, more and more people tried to discover what had happened to it. Working from the writings on Mayan ruins, Charles-Etienne Brasseur decided that it had been destroyed by the eruption of a volcano (opposite).

BUILDING ON A THEORY

Augustus Le Plongeon was a French doctor who had lived for many years in the Yucatán Peninsula of Mexico. He was the first to dig up the Mayan ruins there. He found some pictures on the ruined walls of the city of Chichén-Itzá and connected them with Brasseur's theories.

" . . . the books were about a huge volcanic eruption in an unknown land."

In 1886, Le Plongeon wrote *Sacred Mysteries Among the Mayas and the Quichés 11,500 Years Ago*. In this book, Le Plongeon told the story of Móo, queen of the land of Mu. He wrote: "The country of the hills of mud, the land of Mu, was sacrificed. Being twice upheaved, it disappeared during the night, the basin being continually shaken by volcanic forces. At last the surface gave way, and 10 countries were torn asunder." Le Plongeon went on to say that as the land was ripped apart, various countries "sank with their 64 million inhabitants, 8,060 years before the writing of this book."

There is little doubt that Le Plongeon had Plato's story of Atlantis in mind when he wrote this. In fact Brasseur, too, had connected Atlantis with a myth of the Quichés, who were the Mayas' neighbors. This myth is known as the Popol Vuh. The story tells of a huge lost empire under the ground— not lying beneath the sea.

TALL TALES

The strangest of all stories written about Atlantis came more than 25 years later. It was an article written by Paul Schliemann for the *New York American*. He claimed that he was the grandson of Heinrich Schliemann, a man who had become world famous when he uncovered the ancient city

This is part of a magnificent wall painting found by Augustus Le Plongeon in a temple in the ancient Mayan city of Chichén-Itzá.

These items were found by Heinrich Schliemann in the ancient city of Troy.

of Troy in the 1870s. In his article, Paul Schliemann wrote that his grandfather had left him some papers and a vase with an owl's head on it. Among the papers, said Schliemann, was an account by his grandfather. It told of finding a large bronze vase in the ruins of Troy. Inside were coins and objects. Paul Schliemann claimed that his grandfather had said these items had writing on them that read, "From the King Cronos of Atlantis." Paul Schliemann said: "You can imagine my excitement; here was the first material evidence of that great continent whose legend has lived for ages." He said that he had also read a 4,000-year-old manuscript from a Tibetan monastery. It told how "the Land of the Seven Cities" had been destroyed by an earthquake. Mu, "the priest of Ra," had warned the people that this would take place.

FACT OR FICTION?

After his article first appeared, Schliemann promised to write a book about his discoveries, but that never happened. Nobody ever saw the vase with the owl's head on it, or the manuscript from Tibet, or the other relics. It was later discovered that he was not even the grandson of Heinrich Schliemann. The whole article had been a hoax. However, there were still those who continued to believe in the land of Mu.

Mu and Lemuria

As the hunt for Atlantis continued, it began to appear that there might also be other lost lands.

While Donnelly and Le Plongeon were writing their books about Atlantis, a group of scientists were studying the history of rock formations around the world. They noticed that some rocks and certain fossils that were found in an area of central India were similar to those that could be found in South Africa. These rocks had all been formed around 250 million years ago. The scientists suggested that there might once have been land joining India to the island of Madagascar, and on to South Africa.

ONE VAST CONTINENT

The German scientist Ernst Heinrich Haekel was fascinated by this idea. Unusual small mammals called lemurs are commonly found on the island of Madagascar. However, they are also found in Africa, India, and Malaysia. Haekel suggested that this was evidence that a "land bridge" still existed 70 million years ago, when the first mammals evolved. An English scientist called this land bridge "Lemuria."

In 1908, an American geologist named Frank Taylor came up with the theory that the landmasses of the Earth have gradually drifted apart.

Lemurs (opposite) are found not only in Madagascar, but also in Africa, India, and Malaysia. This led some scientists to believe that there had once been land linking all these places together.

" **Unusual small mammals called lemurs are commonly found on the island of Madagascar.** "

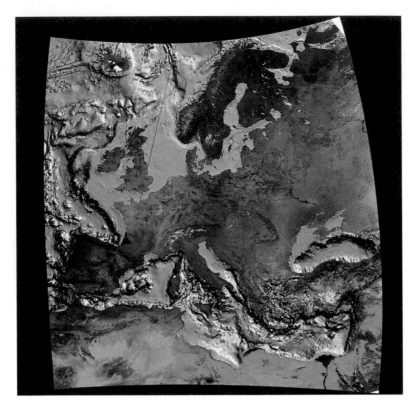

*This hand-tinted satellite map of Europe shows the landscape of the seafloor
(the areas colored silver). A flat, shallow area surrounds Great Britain and
northern Europe. The raised silver areas are actually rough, deep regions
formed by continental drift. Could these areas once have been above water?*

A German scientist, Alfred Wegener, supported this
idea in 1915. For 40 years, few people paid any atten-
tion to such ideas. However, scientists now believe
that all the continents of the world once formed a
single landmass. They call it Pangaea. Gradually, the
land drifted into two great masses, which geologists
call Laurasia and Gondwanaland.

The drift continued until the continents, as we
know them today, were formed. But this was many
millions of years before humankind first appeared on
Earth. The land bridge of Lemuria, however, survived in another way.

In 1888, a woman named Madame Helena Blavatsky published a huge book called *The Secret Doctrine*. Madame Blavatsky had founded a mystical movement called the Theosophical Society, and had visited India in 1879. On her return, she began to write *The Secret Doctrine*. She said it was based on the *Book of Dzyan*, which had been shown to her by the "Brotherhood of Mahatmas," which was a religious community living in Tibet. Madame Blavatsky said that the *Book of Dzyan* had been written in Atlantis.

SEVEN CYCLES

According to Madame Blavatsky, the *Book of Dzyan* tells how life develops through seven cycles, while the development of humankind is through seven "Root," or basic, groups. The third of these groups was said to be the Lemurians. They were hermaphrodites—that is, they were male and female at the same time, like snails—and they reproduced by laying eggs. Some had four arms, and others had an eye in the back of their heads. The people of Atlantis were the fourth Root group. The present human race is supposedly the fifth Root group. The last two have yet to appear.

So now, Lemuria had come into the story of Atlantis. Because *The Secret Doctrine* was so difficult to understand, several writers set out to try

Madame Helena Petrovna Blavatsky. Her book, The Secret Doctrine, *was based on another book that she said had been written in Atlantis.*

to explain the meaning of Madame Blavatsky's book. One was W. Scott-Elliot. His book was called *The Story of Atlantis and The Lost Lemuria*. He said Lemuria was "a great southern continent." It had existed at the time of the dinosaurs. Scott-Elliot described the Lemurians as being 10 to 15 feet (3 to 4.5 m) tall. They had eyes set so far apart that they could see sideways as well as forward—something like a horse. They also had a third eye, which became the pineal gland, a part of the brain, in humans.

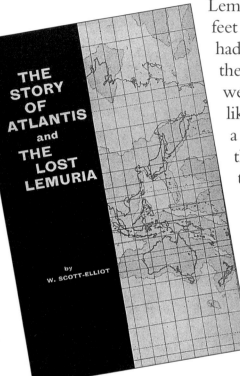

THE STORY OF ATLANTIS and THE LOST LEMURIA

by W. SCOTT-ELLIOT

Here is W. Scott-Elliot's book. In it, he tried to explain Madame Blavatsky's theories.

Scott-Elliot wrote that beings then came down from Venus to teach the Lemurians the arts of civilization. They were taught about weaving, fire, and agriculture, and the science and technology of metal. About 100 million years ago, most of Lemuria began to sink into the sea. The northern part of the continent survived and became Atlantis. Scott-Elliot's book describes Atlantis but reads like science fiction. It is not at all like Plato's account.

THE PLOT THICKENS

Another well-known believer in the land of Lemuria was an Austrian philosopher named Rudolf Steiner. In 1923, he wrote *Lemuria and Atlantis*. In this book

Rudolf Steiner (above) was a member of Madame Blavatsky's Theosophical Society. He wrote a book about Atlantis.

he said that the Lemurians had no memories and did everything on instinct. The people of Atlantis, who followed them, could not reason or calculate, but they had good memories. They had complete control over Earth's forces and even used natural forces to fly aircraft—an ability that had also been described by Scott-Elliot.

FURTHER THEORIES

Soon after the appearance of Steiner's book, "Colonel" James Churchward published *The Lost Continent of Mu*. He said his information came from two sets of tablets. The first set of tablets had come from Mexico. Churchward described the second set as "Naacal tablets written with the Naga symbols." He said that they had been shown to him either in India or in Tibet. Churchward described Mu as being a large continent in the Pacific Ocean. It stretched from Hawaii to the Fiji Islands, and from Easter Island to the Marianas. The population was 64 million, and it was ruled by a priest-emperor called Ra. People from Mu went to settle in Atlantis. Others went to Asia.

Churchward believed that disaster came suddenly to Mu and Atlantis about 13,000 years ago. "Gas belts," huge caves under the Earth, collapsed. The continents sank into the sea, and huge numbers of people were drowned. The survivors crowded onto the tiny islands of Polynesia.

Churchward was old—in his 70s—when he wrote *The Lost Continent of Mu*. He followed it with two more books: *The Children of Mu*, and *The Sacred Symbols of Mu*. There is little doubt that the books came entirely from his imagination. However, he inspired a famous comic strip. This described the adventures of Alley Oop, who dressed in skins, lived in the land of Mu, and fought dinosaurs!

OTHERS TAKE UP THE TALE

Meanwhile interest in Mu, Lemuria, and Atlantis spread among groups who believed in the supernatural. During the 1920s, Edgar Lucien Larkin ran what he called the "Mount Lowe Observatory" in California. This was a great tourist attraction. Larkin had a small telescope, through which he showed visitors the stars. He claimed that with this telescope he had been able to see Mount Shasta, which was 600 miles (900 km) away. Larkin also said that he had watched a thousand Lemurians living in a "mystic village," which was built around a magnificent temple.

Many other unusual societies and organizations also sprang up, all

Here is one of James Churchward's books. Although written as fact, they read like fiction.

of them having something to say about Atlantis and the theories of Madame Blavatsky. Early in the 1930s, Rupert Clymer, from Quakertown, Pennsylvania, published many books that promised his readers the secrets of the original fire-worship of Atlantis. He said the people of Atlantis were highly advanced in scientific and magical matters. They had tried to contact God, but this had upset the Earth's natural forces. The continent sank into the sea.

" . . . he had watched a thousand Lemurians living in a 'mystic village.' "

"TERRIBLE CRYSTALS"

In 1933, the psychic Edgar Cayce had predicted the 1968 discovery of the Bimini Road in the waters off the Bahamas. Cayce worked as a healer. He tried to discover what was wrong with people while he was in a state of trance, or meditation. He said that many surprising things were revealed to him during these trances. The technology of Atlantis, said Cayce, was all based on the "Terrible Crystals." Perhaps this was something that had been taught to the Lemurians by visitors from Venus, if W. Scott-Elliot's theories on the subject are to be believed.

These crystals could draw energy from the stars. As the people of Atlantis became more greedy, they tuned the crystals so that they would give off more power. Unused energy ran off into the ground. Gradually this energy collected to dangerous levels and finally brought about the destruction of Atlantis.

Looking for Atlantis

If Plato's story of Atlantis were true, where could the island continent have been?

In his story of Atlantis, the Greek philosopher Plato gave very clear details about the location of the island continent:

"There was an island situated in front of the Straits [of Gibraltar] that are called by you the Pillars of Hercules. The island was bigger than North Africa and Asia put together and was the way to other islands. From these you might pass to the whole of the opposite continent, which surrounded the true ocean."

AN AFRICAN CONNECTION

Another Greek, who wrote before Plato, was Herodotus. He lived some 2,500 years ago, in the fifth century B.C. Herodotus was a historian, but he had also traveled in many parts of the Near East. He reported some of the stories that he had heard on his travels. He wrote that far to the west there was "a mountain called Atlas. The natives call this mountain the Pillar of Heaven. They themselves take their name from it, being called Atlantes."

There is, indeed, a long range of mountains in North Africa, running through Morocco and Algeria, and into Tunisia. They are called

There were many ideas about where Atlantis might have been. Ancient historians, such as Herodotus and Pliny, wrote of people called the Atlantes, who came from North Africa (opposite).

"The people called the Atlantes lived in the middle of the North African desert."

This is a statue of the giant known as Atlas. According to Greek legend, the gods forced him to hold the sky on his shoulders for all time.

the Atlas Mountains. Greek myths and legends told the story of Atlas, a giant who carried the weight of the sky on his shoulders. According to the Greeks, he did this on Mount Atlas, which is the highest peak of the Atlas Mountains.

Ancient statues of Atlas show him with the weight of the sky on his shoulders in the form of a huge globe. Early books of maps often began with a picture of Atlas. Many historians interested in the ancient world have suggested that Plato came up with the name of Atlantis after reading the stories that Herodotus had written about his travels.

PEOPLE CALLED ATLANTES

Also in the fifth century B.C., a sailor named Hanno set out through the Pillars of Hercules. He sailed along the West African coast. After sailing for many days, he reported that he had found a small island. He called it Kernë.

Nearly 200 years after Plato, Diodorus Siculus, a historian, described a tribe of warlike women called Amazons. They were said to live in the west of North Africa. Diodorus said that these women made war on a people known as the Atlantioi. One of the cities captured by the Amazons was called Kernë.

Then, in the first century A.D., the well-respected Roman historian Pliny wrote his great work called *Natural History*. Writing about Kernë, Pliny noted that, "There is another island situated opposite Mount Atlas, known as Atlantis." However, he also wrote that the "people called Atlantes" lived in the middle of the North African desert.

These writings led some people to believe that Atlantis was not an island continent in the Atlantic Ocean. They decided that it had been a powerful empire in North Africa. A German explorer named Leo Frobenius thought he had discovered Atlantis

Herodotus had written about people called Atlantes in North Africa. This seemed to be confirmed by Pliny. However, this wall painting was found in Mexico. It is said to show the Red god and the god Itzamna, two "gods of the Atlantes."

This mosaic, found in the ruins of the ancient city of Pompeii, shows the Greek philosopher Plato surrounded by a group of his students. Plato was the first to write down the story of the lost continent of Atlantis.

in Nigeria, on the west coast of Africa. He found elephants, a wide variety of plants, natives dressed in blue, and rich deposits of copper ore. All this, he thought, was close to Plato's description of Atlantis. He went on to suggest that, in fact, civilization had begun on a lost continent in the Pacific Ocean. It had then spread from there all over the world.

POSSIBLE EXPLANATIONS

The problem with all these ideas is that they do not fit in with Plato's description. Most of them place Atlantis firmly on dry land, not under the sea.

Researchers went back to the Greek myths. In these myths, the Pillars of Hercules are associated with a place in Spain called Tartessus. Herodotus described how a ship was blown out to sea through the Pillars during a storm. It had finally reached the coast of Spain, near Tartessus, which turned out to be an important trading city. Southern Spain is rich in ores that contain traces of valuable metals. The city of Tartessus seems to have been on an island near the mouth of the present Guadalquivir River, not far from Cadiz.

Nobody has yet found the site of the city of Tartessus. However, a group of German researchers in the 1920s decided that Tartessus was Atlantis. It had certainly been an island beyond the Pillars of Hercules—now the Strait of Gibraltar. It had a rich trade in metals, and there was a large plain behind it, backed by mountains, as described by Plato.

" There are legends of a sunken city off the Brittany coast. . . . "

But Tartessus had not been destroyed by an earthquake. It did not sink suddenly into the sea. The Guadalquivir River brought down vast amounts of mud from the mountains. The island was surrounded by a vast swamp. Mosquitoes bred there, and the citizens became infected with malaria. Slowly, the city had disappeared beneath the mud.

OTHER SUNKEN LANDS

Was Atlantis, in fact, farther away from the Pillars of Hercules? Was it actually somewhere between the coast of Brittany, which is in northwest France, and the coast of Cornwall, which is in southwest England? There are legends of a sunken city off the

Brittany coast, and Cornish legend tells of the lost land of Lyonesse. This land supposedly lay just to the west of Land's End, which is right on the tip of Cornwall. The Isles of Scilly, which are located just a few miles from the tip of Cornwall, are said to be the last remains of the land of Lyonesse.

In Wales, similar tales are told, and the Irish people of Connemara speak of a drowned city off the west coast. One day, it is said, it will rise again, and at the same time Galway will sink.

GHOSTS OF THE PAST

One dark, stormy night in 1946, people on the south side of Galway Bay were shocked to see lights twinkling over the water where the old sunken city was supposed to be. A man who tried to telephone Galway was told by the operator: "There is no reply. They must be all dead over there!" To everyone's relief, a fleet of Spanish fishing boats was seen the following morning. It had been sheltering from a storm.

Heather on the island of Tresco, which is the second largest of the Isles of Scilly group, off Cornwall. These islands are said to be the remains of Lyonesse.

This is the island of Inishtooskert, on Ireland's Atlantic coast, seen from the Dingle Peninsula, County Kerry. Could Atlantis also lie off these shores?

Geologists are all agreed on the fact that Ireland, Great Britain, and France were once a single land-mass. The sea was lower than it is today because much of the world's water was frozen. Even the North Sea, between England and the Netherlands, was a flat plain, with rivers flowing through it. As the ice melted, the sea level rose. The English Channel, between England and France, filled with water that flowed northward to create the North Sea. This process happened between about 7000 and 5400 B.C.

SUNKEN LANDS

These dates fit in quite well with Plato's description of events. In 1935, a well-educated Frenchman named Gidon claimed that Plato had described a land that had once existed between Brittany and

37

These Dutch workers are weaving cut reeds together into low barriers in order to strengthen the banks of the flood dikes. This activity has taken place regularly since the disastrous flooding of the Zuider Zee in A.D. 1282.

Ireland. Gidon claimed that: "Plato's story is based upon a series of floodings like that of the Zuider Zee." The flooding of the Zuider Zee, in Holland, took place in A.D. 1282. The fact is recorded historically. A plain of dry land lay below sea level, but was protected by natural banks of higher land. During a tremendous storm, the seawater broke through and flooded the whole area in a single day. The Dutch constructed a series of flood dikes, which are like canals or ditches, and continue to pump the water off the land to the present day.

WORLDS IN COLLISION

In 1950, Immanuel Velikovsky published his book *Worlds in Collision*. He claimed that a huge comet had come close to the Earth. It caused the destruction of Atlantis and many other worldwide changes.

38

It then moved away to become the planet Venus. Velikovsky wrote "of forests burning and swept away, of dust, stones, fire, and ashes falling from the sky. Of mountains melting like wax, of lava flowing . . . . Of shaking ground and destroyed cities, of humans seeking refuge in caverns . . . . Of oceans upheaved and falling on the land, of tidal waves moving toward the poles and back."

A GRAIN OF TRUTH

Astronomers say that there is no evidence at all for Velikovsky's theories. However, it is now agreed that huge meteors have struck the Earth in the distant past, causing dramatic changes.

One of the biggest of these struck Yucatán in southeastern Mexico. It has often been suggested that this area was part of the original Atlantean empire. But this disaster was many millions of years before humankind existed. Some people think that the dust cloud it produced wiped out the dinosaurs.

" *Of shaking ground and destroyed cities, of humans seeking refuge in caverns.*"

IMMANUEL VELIKOVSKY

All these theories about the possible site of Atlantis were interesting, but they had no historical backing. Many archaeologists and other experts on ancient history decided to take another closer look at Plato's story. Then, some 30 years ago, they came up with what could be the true explanation.

Was This the Real Atlantis?

Plato said that the destruction of Atlantis had occurred around 10,000 B.C. But the story had come to him from his great-grandfather, who had been told it by the Greek lawmaker Solon. Solon was born around 640 B.C., and he had heard the story from an old Egyptian priest. So could the date be relied upon, or was somebody mistaken?

There is also confusion about the huge distances described by Plato. If the story of Atlantis is true, perhaps Plato had only guessed that it lay beyond the Pillars of Hercules. Perhaps he just could not imagine that the calm waters of the Mediterranean Sea covered a sunken continent.

CLUES IN THE MEDITERRANEAN

There is no mention of Atlantis in Greek literature before Plato. However, Homer's *Odyssey* (written around 600 B.C.) describes a mysterious island called Skeria. Homer's description sounds very like Atlantis. The royal palace had doors of solid gold, and the walls were made of bronze. There was a temple to Poseidon, the sea god. The city had a wall all around, and a large sea harbor. The mountains had many springs

The remains of the Minoan palace of Knossos, on the island of Crete (opposite). It is now almost certain that the Greek islands hold the key to the mystery of the lost world of Atlantis.

40

"The destruction of Thera and Minoan Crete seems to have been the true story of Atlantis."

and rivers, and the ground was full of precious metals. But where was Skeria? Did Homer imagine it, or was it a real place? In 1915, an expert named Walter Leaf became convinced that Skeria was Atlantis, and he linked it with the Greek island of Crete. Modern research suggests that he was nearly right.

"It was clear that the ancient civilization of Crete had been important."

At the beginning of the 20th century, the English archaeologist Sir Arthur Evans decided to investigate by digging on Crete. He made an amazing discovery.

A WHOLE LOST CIVILIZATION

Ancient Greek legends told the story of Minos, king of Crete. His wife was Pasiphaë, and they lived in the palace of Knossos. Poseidon sent King Minos a beautiful white bull to be sacrificed. But Minos kept it alive. Poseidon was angry and made Pasiphaë fall in love with the bull. She gave birth to a creature called the Minotaur, which had the head of a bull and the body of a man. The Minotaur was kept in a maze of passages called the labyrinth. When the son of Minos was murdered by people from Athens, King Minos demanded that seven young men and seven young women be sent to Crete from Athens each year. They were locked up with the Minotaur, which killed them.

Until Sir Arthur Evans began digging, everybody thought this story was just a myth. But Evans soon uncovered a magnificent palace at Knossos. Most surprisingly, wall paintings showed young men and women leaping over a charging bull—and the kings of Atlantis were said to have sacrificed a bull to Poseidon each year. More ruins were discovered. All looked as if they had been suddenly destroyed by fire.

It was clear that the ancient civilization of Crete had been important. It is now called the "Minoan" civilization, after king Minos, and is thought to have lasted from about 3000 to 1450 B .C . But how could Crete be Atlantis? Plato said the island was destroyed nearly 10,000 years before his time—not 1,000 years. But then, in 1967, new information came to light.

FORCES OF NATURE

The story began back in 1939, when Greek archae-ologist Spyridon Marinatos came across ash from a volcano on the north coast of Crete. He wondered whether the Minoan civilization had been destroyed by a natural disaster. But then World War II broke out, with the German occupation of Greece, and the civil war that followed. Marinatos had to wait nearly 30 years to test his theory.

Elk walk through a forest, which was buried under thick layers of ash after the eruption of the volcano on Mount Saint Helens, Washington State, in 1980.

The popular picture of a volcanic eruption is of streams of red-hot lava rushing down a mountainside. But eruptions can be more violent than this. There can be a huge explosion, which hurls thousands of tons of ash—known as "tephra"—into the air. This was what happened when the volcano on Mount Saint Helens, in Washington State, erupted in 1980. The ash rose 60,000 feet (18,300 m) and drifted for hundreds of miles.

There is another result of the eruption of a volcano that can be just as destructive. This is the tidal wave, or "tsunami." Land movement below the sea can produce huge waves, some traveling at up to 400 miles per hour (mph) (644 kilometers per hour [kmph]). When Krakatau, in Indonesia, exploded in 1883, great waves struck the coasts of Java and Sumatra. They were over 100 feet (30 m) high. More than 36,000 people were drowned. Perhaps something like this happened to Atlantis.

THERA EXPLODES

Less than 100 miles (161 km) north of Crete are a number of small islands. One of these is Thera. Around 20,000 years ago it was a round volcanic island with a peak 5,000 feet (1,525 m) high. But in about 1450 B.C., Thera exploded. The central part of the island

The island of Thera. The harbor was created in about 1450 B.C., when the center of the island collapsed after a volcanic explosion.

collapsed, leaving a deep basin about 6 miles (10 km) wide. The sea rushed in to fill the space. The ash that fell on the surrounding land was nearly 200 feet (60 m) thick. Strong winds then carried the ash to the southeast, perhaps even as far as Egypt.

DEATH AND DESTRUCTION

The explosion on the island of Thera also caused huge tidal waves that seriously damaged the north coast of Crete. Nobody lived on Thera for centuries afterward, but eventually people were able to settle there again. Today, Thera is a crescent-shaped island. Sheer cliffs some 800 feet (244 m) high surround the basin where the sea rushed in.

"Volcanic ash fell over Crete. It blocked out the sun, and there was no light."

In 1967, Spyridon Marinatos went to Thera to find out whether people had lived there before the eruption. He dug in the volcanic ash at a settlement on Thera and soon uncovered the remains of an ancient port. Now we can guess what happened in 1450 B.C.

First, there were earthquakes. Fires would have started underground. Then, the volcano under Thera exploded. The first tidal wave would have struck the north coast of Crete within an hour of the first earthquakes. There is evidence to support this. Different pieces of the same stone lamp were found in the ruins of houses 100 feet (30 m) apart. This is most likely to have been caused by a great wave of water.

After this, volcanic ash began to fall all over Crete. It blocked out the sun, and there was no light. Experts have worked out that the explosion could have been heard as far as 1,000 miles (1,609 km) away. Nothing could grow. The water was full of ash, and the surviving people could not drink it. Buildings were damaged or destroyed. The Minoan way of life was over.

This Minoan pottery, identical to that found on Crete, was discovered at Akrotiri.

WAS THIS ATLANTIS?

The destruction of Thera and Minoan Crete seems to have been the true story of Atlantis. But what of the date and distances given in Plato's story? The eruption of Thera took place about 900 years before the time of Solon, rather than 9,000 years. And it is also an interesting fact that the distance of the Pillars of Hercules from Egypt is almost exactly 10 times the distance of Thera from Egypt.

Some experts have suggested that the ancient Egyptians had made a mistake and multiplied both figures by 10. On the other hand, perhaps the old priest himself had multiplied the figures by 10 in order to make the story more exciting. Or perhaps it was Plato himself who was responsible. The truth may never be known.

Glossary

archaeologist A person who studies the art and dwellings of past human life.

calculate To work out, usually by using mathematical methods.

civilization Advanced human development in a particular time or place. "The Aztec civilization."

continent A great landmass such as North America, Africa, or Asia.

earthquake A sudden shaking of the Earth's surface.

expeditions Trips or journeys to find out about something.

geologists Scientists who study the structure of the Earth.

historian A person who studies or writes about history.

ice age A period of time when Earth was covered with ice. There have been several ice ages.

inhabitants People or animals living in a particular place.

inscriptions Writing scratched into the surface of stone.

instinct The ability to act in a certain way without thinking.

lava Hot, liquid rock.

malaria A disease caused by the bite of certain mosquitoes.

manuscript An author's typed or handwritten book or article.

meteor Matter in space that burns up if it enters Earth's atmosphere.

monastery A building where monks live. Nuns live in convents.

mosaic A picture or design created from pieces of colored glass or stone.

mummies Bodies that have been stopped from decaying. This was common practice in ancient Egypt.

mystical Matters having to do with spiritual or religious mysteries.

philosopher Someone who studies the nature and meaning of life.

propositions Opinions put forward for consideration by others.

psychic A person who claims to be able to see into the future, or who has other unexplained mind powers.

theory An unproven idea.

tidal wave A huge wave sometimes caused by an undersea earthquake.

trance A sleeplike condition of the mind while a person is awake.

translate To put speech or writing into another language.

volcanic eruptions The sudden, explosive throwing out of lava, ash, and gases from a volcano.

Index

Further Reading

Barber, Nicola. *The Search for Lost Cities*, "Treasure Hunters" series. Raintree Steck-Vaughn, 1998

Brouwer, Sigmund. *Sunrise at the Mayan Temple*, "Accidental Detective" series. Chariot Victor, 1995

Keller, Kent. *The Mayan Mystery*, "Choice Adventures" series. Tyndale, 1994

Morris, Gilbert. *The Gates of Neptune*, "Seven Sleepers" series. Moody, 1994

Thompson, Colin. *Looking for Atlantis*. Random House Books, 1997